ALAN TOMS

Where is God's House Today?

✝ **HAYES**
PRESS Christian Publisher

Contents

PROLOGUE

Where is God's House Today? Our question is not about the Father's house in Heaven. The Lord Jesus spoke of that when He said in John 14 verse 2: "In my Father's house are many rooms ... I go to prepare a place for you." Everyone who knows Christ as Saviour is assured of a place in His Father's house in Heaven. The prospect is glorious. Rather our question is about God's house on earth, about which the Bible has so much to say. "Will God indeed dwell with man on the earth?" (2 Chronicles 6:18), King Solomon asked in wonder. The answer is 'Yes', amazing as it is to human minds. We cannot read our Bibles without coming to that conclusion, for again and again God speaks in His word about His house.

In the Old Testament the subject of God's house runs from Genesis to Malachi, and from Matthew to Revelation it is everywhere in the New Testament. One essential difference between the two is that before the death of the Lord Jesus, God lived in a physical house, but when the veil of the temple was torn in two God signified the end of the old order and the beginning of the new. When the Holy Spirit descended on the day of Pentecost we see the beginning of God's spiritual house. The apostle Peter wrote about disciples of the Lord Jesus being built together as

1

living stones into a spiritual house where as a holy priesthood they would serve God by offering up spiritual sacrifices (1 Peter 2:5), from which we learn that it is the place of collective worship for believers today. The apostle Paul wrote of the same spiritual house when he gave Timothy instructions about behaviour that was in keeping with it (1 Timothy 3:15), so we see that it affects the practical daily life of the disciple.

And when Paul wrote to the Ephesians, he referred to buildings, of which the company of disciples in the Church of God in Ephesus was one. These 'buildings' being joined together and growing into a holy temple in the Lord (Ephesians 2:21), show us that the house of God in the New Testament is made up of groups of believers, known and identified as Churches of God, and joined together as one thing. In the days of the apostles, companies of disciples were brought together as Churches of God. They formed God's house on earth, and God dwelt in them collectively by His Spirit (1 Corinthians 3:16).

These churches are not to be confused with the Church which is Christ's body, which is composed of all born-again persons from the day of Pentecost to the coming again of the Lord Jesus. Most of the members of His Body are now in heaven, of course, but those who are still alive on earth have the privilege of obeying the word of the Lord and being gathered with like-minded disciples in a local church of God.

That was how it worked in the days of the apostles. Members of the Church which is His Body, submitting to immersion baptism in acknowledgement of Christ as Lord, were then added together with other disciples to form a testimony for God in the town or

2

city where they lived. And if it was so then, we must conclude that the same is possible today, for the word of God has not changed. That immediately introduces us to questions of urgent and vital interest. If God is dwelling among men on earth today, where is His dwelling place? And how may I be sure of a place in it?

This book has been written because believers want to know the answers to these questions. In it we shall range through the Scriptures, looking firstly at the Old Testament, to learn its lessons. We remember that "whatever was written in former days was written for our instruction" (Romans 15:4) and the tabernacle which Moses built, for example, is said in the New Testament to be a symbol or parable for the present time (Hebrews 9:9). As we then apply these lessons to what is written in the New Testament, let us ask that God's Holy Spirit will make clear to us the lessons He wants us to learn in regard to the worship and service of. God today. We will begin where God begins, in the book of Genesis.

Review

1. What is the essential difference between God's house in the Old Testament and the New
2. What do we learn from 1 Peter 2:5 about (a) the composition of God's house, (b) its construction and (c) its function?

JACOB AND THE HOUSE OF GOD

"This is none other than the house of God" (Genesis 28:17). So said Jacob when God revealed Himself to him in a special way when he was on his long journey to his uncle. He was running for his life, to escape his brother's anger. But God had His eye on him. Although Jacob was unaware of it at the time, God was directing his journey and He brought him one evening at sunset to a very special place. Genesis 28 verses 10 to 22 give us the account. It says "He came to a certain place." The margin of the Revised Version Bible says "the place" and in that place he lay down to sleep with a stone for a pillow.

During the night God spoke to him, and he saw a ladder set up on earth, the top of which reached to heaven, and angels of God ascending and descending on it. In the morning when he woke he was conscious of the presence of God in a way he had not felt it before. "Surely the Lord is in this place," he said; "this is none other than the house of God, and this is the gate of heaven!" And that is the very first mention in our Bibles of this important subject of the house of God.

Jacob called the place Bethel – 'beth' meaning house, and 'El', the name of God – i.e. the house of God. In the book of Genesis we have the beginning of many subjects which are later expanded in other parts of the Scriptures. But very often in the Genesis reference, where the subject is presented in embryo form, we gather basic principles. So it is with the subject of God's house.

The Place

This was a place which was special to God. Six times in the short passage it is called "the place" or "this place." There was nothing to distinguish it from other places when Jacob arrived; although when he left he set up his stony pillow as a pillar and poured oil on the top of it, to mark the spot. Other men would pass it by without a thought. The passage says the name of the place had been Luz previously, and doubtless it always would be Luz as far as most people were concerned. It was just another place along the way. But not so to Jacob. It held memories for him which were forever precious. It was the place where he found God! And God gave him a new revelation of Himself. He became the God of Bethel to Jacob that day, and that fresh and further knowledge of God was something that deeply blessed Jacob all the rest of his life.

So there was a place away back in those early days where God revealed Himself in a particular way. There was no building there, nothing to mark it out, but God was there, and to it He later brought men, and women, who had hearts to understand. Many passed it by without a second thought, but some stayed and met with God, and it brought a new dimension into their lives.

In our experience it is the same today. Many dismiss the subject as unimportant, even among born-again people. Other things fill their thoughts and they pass on their way. But please take the time and trouble to work through this book, checking the Bible references as you do, to ensure that the facts are Bible-based, and to face the question of whether this is something precious to God, and which should claim your close attention.

Basic Principles

From a careful study of Genesis 28, we learn some fundamental principles about God's house and among the most obvious are the following. The ladder Jacob saw was set up on earth, although its top reached to heaven, and above it stood the Lord. The house of God is a place based on earth, and the Lord stands above it, the One in authority over it. In the New Testament the Lord Jesus is called "Son over His own house" (Hebrews 3:6, Revised Version). It is the place where His authority is acknowledged and His word obeyed. It is the gate of heaven. When men wanted to approach God it was to His house they came. Jacob came to this place for a fresh and fuller revelation of God. He knew Him previously as the God of Abraham and of Isaac, as the covenant-keeping God, faithful to His spoken word.

But now he knew Him as the God of Bethel, the God of the house of God. It was an awesome experience in one sense, for he felt the holiness of God that day as never before, but he went away blessed in his heart. Jacob never forgot Bethel and when God called him back to it on his return journey, his first thought was to put right things that were wrong in his family life. "Holiness befits your house, O LORD" (Psalm 93:5), and although Jacob

6

lived hundreds of years before the psalmist wrote these words, he knew the truth of them.

Review

1. What was special about the place where Jacob lay down to sleep?
2. What fresh revelation of God did he receive there?
3. Name three basic principles about the house of God which stand out in this account of Jacob's encounter with God.

GOD'S DESIRE FOR A DWELLING PLACE

I n Genesis, God was dealing with individuals. In Exodus He took Jacob's family and, beginning with his twelve sons, formed them into a nation. With the formation of that nation the subject we are considering takes a leap forward. From its embryo beginning in Genesis it now takes visible shape and we are introduced to God's first physical house, the tabernacle which was built in the desert. "Let them make Me a sanctuary" is a quotation from Exodus 25:8. So the desire for a house on earth originated with God; it was at His request it was built, although the privilege of providing the materials and of constructing it under Moses' leadership was given to Israel. They had just been constituted a nation and we must carefully notice the experiences through which they had to pass before God could make His remarkable request to them.

Redemption

They had been slaves in Egypt, but God, remembering His promise to Abraham, Isaac and Jacob, sent Moses to deliver them from slavery. The story is a gripping one of how Egypt's Pharaoh matched his power against the almighty power of God, only to find in the end that God is stronger than all His enemies. Proud Pharaoh and his army lay buried in the depths of the Red Sea and the people of Israel stood on the far shore singing God's praise. They had been redeemed from slavery by the blood of the Passover lambs and by God's power. And therein lies the great truth of redemption which runs like a scarlet cord throughout the Scriptures. There could have been no redemption for sinners apart from the blood of Christ shed at Calvary, and the mighty power of God displayed on that first resurrection morning. Christ "was delivered up for our trespasses, and raised for our justification" (Romans 4:25).

Baptism

From Egypt they came to the Red Sea where "all were baptized into Moses in the cloud and in the sea" (1 Corinthians 10:2). It was a true figure of believers' baptism, for they literally passed through a watery grave with walls of water on either side. As Israel was identified with Moses as their leader, so we are identified with our Leader in His death and resurrection. We reckon ourselves dead to sin and alive to God in Christ Jesus. And they came up singing their song of deliverance on the other shore; the first song recorded in the scriptures.

Promised Obedience

From that point, God led them to Mount Sinai where He gave them a law to keep. The ten commandments were the basis of it, although there was much more involved, for it touched every area of their lives. Moses brought it down from Sinai where he met God and when he had read it to them they said, "All that the

LORD has spoken we will do, and we will be obedient" (Exodus 24:7). At that stage Moses took blood, which he called the blood of the covenant, and sprinkled it first on the book and then on the people. And the people became the people of the book. To this Hebrews 9:19, 20 refers. They had pledged their obedience to the Lord.

And then God said, "Speak to the children of Israel, that they bring Me an offering. From everyone who brings it willingly with his heart you shall take My offering ... and let them make Me a sanctuary; that I may dwell among them" (Exodus 25:2,8, Revised Version). This brings us to the very heart of our subject. The great desire of God was actually taking shape in the hands of men. The materials were gathered, an abundant supply, and specially gifted men commenced the intricate work of building the house and the furniture according to the pattern Moses had received from God. Many of the people of this new nation helped in its preparation; the women in their tents weaving the cloth, the men in the work of construction.

But please notice that before the work began, before even God made His request, certain conditions had been fulfilled. They had been redeemed by blood, baptized in water and pledged to obedience to all that the Lord had spoken. In token of the covenant God had made with them, they were sprinkled with blood.

The New Testament Parallel

We turn to our New Testament scriptures to see a clear parallel, for the apostle Peter writes to God's elect who had been redeemed with precious blood (1 Peter 1:18,19) and baptized in water in acknowledgement of the claims of their risen Master (1 Peter 3:21), "for obedience to Jesus Christ and for sprinkling with his blood" (1 Peter 1:2). We will later show the important difference between being "redeemed with precious blood" and the "sprinkling with his blood."

Under the old covenant God had a physical house where the worship and service of His people was centred. But at the death and resurrection of the Lord Jesus, God made a break with the old and introduced something new. Now, as Stephen and Paul both remind us, "the Most High does not dwell in houses made with hands" (Acts 7:48, 17:24). His house today is composed of disciples, described as stones, who have received life from Christ, the chief corner stone, and are together to form both God's house where dwells and His sanctuary where He is and served.

1 Peter 2:5 (Revised Version) is a key verse: "You also, as living stones, are being built up a spiritual house, a holy priesthood, to offer up spiritual sacrifices, acceptable to God through Jesus Christ." Clearly the emphasis now is on living stones, a spiritual house and spiritual sacrifices. But basic principles do not change and those who comprise God's house today are first of all redeemed by blood, then baptized in water and pledged to obedience to the word of the Lord, which all agrees so completely with the final commission of our Lord Jesus before He returned

11

to heaven:

> "*And Jesus came and said to them, 'All authority in heaven and on earth has been given to me. Go therefore and make disciples of all nations, baptizing them in the name of the Father and of the Son and of the Holy Spirit, teaching them to observe all that I have commanded you. And behold, I am with you always, to the end of the age'* (Matthew 28:18-20).

This commission has never been repealed. It holds good today, binding on all who love our Lord Jesus and want to please Him. It might be well to pause at this point and ask ourselves to what extent are we observing the "all" He has commanded us. We recognise, of course, that His commandments reach us through His own words and the writings of His apostles. So the whole of the New Testament scriptures is involved, "the faith which was once for all delivered to the saints" (Jude 3). Those of us who are His disciples are committed to do our utmost, by the daily help of the Holy Spirit, to give full expression to His commandments in the way we live and serve.

Review

1. What three experiences did the children of Israel pass through before God requested that they build Him a sanctuary?
2. List three New Testament verses which make it clear that these same three experiences are essential if we are to build God's house today?

3. Pick out the equivalent of these three experiences in the great commission of Matthew 28:18-20. If you wish, use three columns to set out the points in each case.

BUILDING TO A PATTERN

"See to it that you make them according to the pattern" (Exodus 25:40, Revised Version). The words are taken from God's instruction to Moses, who was later described as faithful in all God's house as a servant. That was a high commendation. Moses was chosen for a very responsible task. When God called him to the mountain to meet Him, He knew He was dealing with a man who would be absolutely trustworthy. He showed him a pattern; for what Moses was to build in the desert represented something in heaven. A heavy responsibility rested upon him as he descended the mountain to the people and the leaders of Israel, to convey to them what he had seen, and inspire them with the tremendous importance of the job they had in hand. God could not have been more insistent about keeping to the pattern, for several times He repeated the instruction to make all things according to the pattern.

All things! From the main construction of the tabernacle building down to the tiny detail in some of the furniture. Everything had to be according to the mind of God. There was no room for human ideas. It was to be God's house and He was the Architect, although men were privileged to do the building. And a high privilege it was to have a part in the construction of a building which the eternal God was to make His dwelling place. It is to the credit of all who helped (and there must have been thousands of them) that they carried the work through perfectly; for when the task was completed the glory of the Lord filled the tabernacle. God was completely satisfied. Everything was according to the pattern. And the pillar of cloud by day, and of fire by night, was a constant reminder that the living God was actually dwelling among them.

The words roll off the pen so easily, but what a tremendous truth they convey - the divine Being, while still occupying Heaven's throne, was actually condescending to live among His people on earth. He had pitched His tent in the centre of their tents. They were living, around the dwelling place of God. No wonder Moses said, as he reviewed God's dealings with them, "what great nation is there that has a god so near to it, as the LORD our God is to us," (Deuteronomy 4:7). There was no other nation! No one else shared the privilege. It belonged exclusively to Israel, not because they were greater in number than any other nation, for actually they were fewer, but because God loved them.

The Service of God

One of the jewels in Israel's crown was the service of God (Romans 9:4) and that service was inseparably linked with the house of God. They brought their gifts and sacrifices to God's altar, at the time when incense was burned in the holy place. Their whole life revolved around God's house, at least for the godly Israelite. It was not only the place where God lived among them, but also where they met Him; the very gate of heaven, as Jacob had earlier recognised. There was no part of their service, whether upward to God, or outward to men, which was not associated with God's house.

Has this no voice for us today? Surely it has. Turning to our New Testament scriptures, we find that the service of God in the days of the apostles was all associated with God's spiritual house. As His house, composed of living stones built together, a holy priesthood serves, offering up spiritual sacrifices, and from His house a royal priesthood proclaims "the excellencies of Him Who called you out of darkness into His marvellous light" (1 Peter 2:5,9). Just as in the physical house, so in the spiritual, God has provided the pattern for its building. The apostle Paul received it directly from the Lord Jesus. Into Arabia he went, possibly to the very place where Moses was given the pattern of God's physical house. And not only did he devote a lifetime of tireless service building to it himself, but he also passed it on to others: "Follow the pattern of sound words that you have heard from me" was one of his final instructions to the young man Timothy (2 Timothy 1:13).

The other apostles had of course received it earlier, directly from the Lord Jesus, during the forty days he appeared to them before He finally ascended to His Father. During those days He was spelling out the pattern of their service as they went out to make disciples and baptize them and teach them all things He had commanded them. And what resulted?

Building to the Pattern

The book of the Acts is an account of the Churches which sprang up as the word of God was carried out. Beginning in Jerusalem at Pentecost and spreading throughout Judea into Samaria, the word eventually reached Antioch in Syria. From this centre the apostle and his companions were commanded to service far and wide. Everywhere they went they preached the Gospel, and the converts gathered together into churches of God those obedient to their teaching. That is how God's spiritual house took shape - individual living stones were built in churches of God. "You are God's building" (1 Corinthians 3:9) wrote the apostle Paul to church of God in Corinth (1 Corinthians 1:2). And each building was to the same pattern, for the teaching was the same wherever he went. Paul was at pains to emphasise that point:

"As I teach ... everywhere in every church" (1 Corinthians 4:17).

"This is my rule in all the churches" (1 Corinthians 7:17).

And 'all the churches' together formed God's house, as Ephesians 2:21-22 (Revised Version) teaches: "Each several building, fitly framed together, groweth into a holy temple in the Lord; in whom ye also are builded together for a habitation of God in the Spirit." In the Revised Version Bible with marginal references you will notice that "every building" is said to be an alternative translation of the words "each several building." The King James Authorised Version expressed it that "all the building," as an integrated structure, grows into a holy temple in the Lord.

Certainly God has had only one house at any one time, and in New Testament days the churches of God together provided that dwelling place for God, in answer to the Master's prayer before He died, "That they may all be one." And in His prayer He gave us the key to its possibility when He said, "Sanctify them in the truth: your word is truth" (John 17:17). Obedience to the truth is the only way such unity is possible.

Word of God or Tradition of Men?

Believers in the Lord Jesus are scattered in so many different denominations today that new converts are often confused as to where God wants them to worship and serve Him. What is the reason? Is it not because some have introduced their own ideas into the service of God? This is not new, for the Lord Jesus accused the Pharisees and scribes of doing the very same thing. They made void the word of God by their tradition, He said. It is a sobering thought that it is possible for us today, who love the Lord Jesus, to serve God according to traditions rather the clear pattern of His word.

Let me illustrate what I mean. Take one example of men's traditions. What of the doctrine of baptismal regeneration which is taught in so many churches? Nowhere in the Scriptures is the sprinkling of infants (or adults) even hinted at, and the suggestion that by its means the infant becomes a child of God in so far removed from scriptural truth it is frightening to contemplate. Only through faith in Christ can a person become a child of God. John 1:12 makes that abundantly clear. Is it according to the pattern that the responsibility for dispensing the emblems at the communion service should be in the hands of an ordained man only?

And how often should this service, the breaking of the bread, be kept? Acts 20:7 indicates the early disciples kept it every Lord's day. And so we could go on. But enough has been said to make the point that the traditions of men can very easily take the place of the word of God. "Everything according to the pattern" (Hebrews 8:5) and "all that I have commanded you" (Matthew 28:20) are still His plain word. It remains only for me to ask that you examine the practices of your church by the word of God, and see if they are the traditions of men or according to the pattern. Of the believers in Rome it is written they obeyed from the heart the standard of teaching to which they were committed (Romans 6:17). Can God say that about you and me?

Review

1. What did the pillar of cloud by day and of fire by night signify?
2. "God pitched His tent in the centre of their tents" is a quote from this chapter. What is so remarkable about that fact?
3. Moses received the pattern for the tabernacle. Who received the pattern for God's spiritual house? Support your answer with spiritual references.
4. Who comprises God's spiritual house today? What is its composition?

GOD'S REST AND THE PLACE OF HIS NAME

After 40 years of desert wandering, Joshua led the people of God into the promised land. And the ark of God went with them, carried on the shoulders of the Levites. Its new home was in Shiloh, a very central position in the land. "The children of Israel assembled together at Shiloh, and set up the tabernacle of meeting there" (Joshua 18:1, Revised Version). That was another name for the tabernacle. It was the tent where God met with His people. God looked back with great affection on Shiloh. Years later, through the prophet Jeremiah He spoke of "My place that was in Shiloh, where I made My name dwell at first" (Jeremiah 7:12). His first place of rest in the land. God never forgot it. And from those same words which God spoke through Jeremiah there shines another shaft of light on this important subject.

God puts His name where He lives and Israel were to come and worship Him there and nowhere else. God's instruction on the point was clear and emphatic: "Take care that you do not offer your burnt offerings at any place that you see, but at the place that the LORD will choose in one of your tribes, there you shall offer your burnt offerings, and there you shall do all that I am commanding you" (Deuteronomy 12:13-14). Three times a year all the males were to go up to God's house to worship Him. God promised to protect their homes and their families during their absence and they took their gifts and sacrifices, or money to purchase them on their arrival.

At such times the highways leading to God's house would be thronged with people, singing together as they went. For some it was a longer journey than others, depending on their proximity to the place where God had put His name. But that did not matter. God's word was plain. There was one place where they were to serve Him, and to that place they must go.

Fellowship Today

God's spiritual house today is not confined to one place. In New Testament times it was composed, as we have seen, of disciples of the Lord Jesus who, though scattered throughout the world, were joined together in churches of God, where the commandments of the Lord Jesus were of first importance. Not one place, physically speaking, but one spiritual unity, of which John 11:52 speaks. One of the great purposes of the death of Christ was that He might gather together into one (or one thing) the children of God that are scattered abroad. For this the Lord Jesus prayed "that they may all be one" (John 17:21,22,23). It is obviously something exceedingly precious to God.

We pause to make the point clear, for it is important that we grasp it. When James stood up at the Jerusalem conference in Acts 15, he referred to this very thing when he said "Simeon has related how God first visited the Gentiles, to take from

21

them a people for his name" (Acts 15:14). From the day of Pentecost onwards God began to do that very thing, to call out from Gentile nations men and women who would obey His word and be gathered together as a people upon whom He could put His name. In the book of Acts we see God at work through His servants as they preached the gospel, taught the converts, and then gathered together those who were obedient to the word of the Lord.

And where were they gathered? In churches of God. The first was in Jerusalem. "I persecuted the church of God," Paul said (Galatians 1:13). And they spread throughout Judea – "the churches of God ... which are in Judea" (1 Thessalonians 2:14). Each church that came into existence as the work spread was called by the same name, e.g. "the church of God in Corinth" (1 Corinthians 1:2; 2 Corinthians 1:1) or whatever the name of the town or city might be. God was gathering out His own special people (Titus 2:14) and He was putting His name on them. They were "of God" because they were built according to His pattern. By His word they came into being.

And as we have seen that was the place where God was content to dwell. "What kind of house will you build for Me? says the Lord, or what is the place of My rest?" (Acts 7:49). God can only rest where His will is done and in the days of the apostles that was in churches of God. In those days new converts would be in no doubt where they should worship God. It was as plain as in the days when His house was in Shiloh. Nobody questioned going to Shiloh, for that was where God had put His name. And in New Testament times we have seen that it was equally plain, and it remains our pattern for today. The churches of God were called by His name. In the churches of God they would worship the Lord.

The churches of God together formed God's house, and there a holy priesthood served, offering up spiritual sacrifices. From that same centre a royal priesthood went out carrying the word of the living God to men and nations around.

Review

1. From Jeremiah 7:12 what do we learn from God's reference to 'My place' and 'My Name'? What is the connection between them?
2. How many times in Deuteronomy 12 does God repeat the instruction that they were to bring their offerings only to the place of His choice? What do we learn from this repetition?
3. In what way does God put His name on His people today?

UNITY IN GOD'S DWELLING PLACE

We must at this point examine the statement that in New Testament times the churches of God together formed God's house. Were they together in a fellowship of assemblies so close that God viewed them as one? And if so, what kept them together? These are important questions.

"The tabernacle shall be one" was God's instruction to Moses in connection with the building of His sanctuary. It is worth noticing that when God speaks of the tabernacle He is referring in this context not to the whole structure, but to the ten curtains which were made of fine twined linen, blue, purple and scarlet with the cherubim. The curtains were made of ten equal parts, five of which were coupled together and the other five likewise. Then the two sets were joined by fifty clasps of gold, and so the tabernacle was one. It was a composite unity made up of equal parts joined together and we draw attention to it because we believe that God wishes us to learn from such important details.

"That they may all be one" was obviously a great burden on the Master's heart as He prayed to His Father the night before He died. Three times He spoke about it, "that they may be one" (John 17:21, 22, 23). As we follow the progress of the work recorded in the Acts of the Apostles we can see that His prayer was answered in those early days, for the churches of God were linked together in an obvious unity which the world could see. It was a unity which came out of obedience to God's word.

"Sanctify them in the truth; your word is truth" (John 17:17).

As each disciple became obedient from his heart to the pattern of teaching presented to him, he found his place in a church of God. And each church was built to the same pattern, believing and practising the same things as we have already noted.

"If any one is inclined to be contentious, we have no such practice, nor do the churches of God" (1 Corinthians 11:16).

The churches of God were 'fitly framed' together into a corporate whole, which was carefully maintained as one by a united elderhood. Let us look more closely at this, for some see the local assembly as an autonomous unit, rather than being linked together in a fellowship of assemblies. But what do the scriptures teach on the subject?

Churches Together in Provinces

1 Thessalonians 2:14 refers to the churches of God in Judea and we know that by this time there were many churches there. When the disciples in Antioch heard of the famine in Judea, they collected and sent a gift for their relief by hand of Barnabas and Saul. It was delivered by elders of the churches, so not only were churches linked together but served by a united elderhood.

25

Indeed as we shall see, that was how the unity was maintained.

When the apostle Paul wanted to take Timothy with him in the full-time service of the Lord, he consulted not only with the brethren in Timothy's home church but with the leaders of the two neighbouring assemblies also. The elders acted together by laying their hands upon him, as 1 Timothy 4:14 shows. And to those same churches of Galatia one letter was addressed (Galatians 1:2). How would it have been circulated had they not been together in fellowship?

Colossians 4:12,13 presents a lovely picture of assemblies linked together, in the reference to Epaphras, Paul's fellow-prisoner. He belonged to the church in Colossae and had been used in the making of many of the disciples there. How he came to be a prisoner is not revealed. Far away in Rome he longed for the disciples in his home assembly, and he prayed for them. And also for the neighbouring assemblies of Laodicea and Hierapolis. And the apostle Paul asked (verse 16) that the letter he was writing to Colossae be read also in Laodicea and that the Laodicean letter be read by the Colossians. Surely that indicates a very close bond between them.

Then what about the churches of Macedonia (2 Corinthians 8:1), whose generous giving was so highly commended by the apostle? Three of them we know, Philippi, Beroea and Thessalonica; and Paul linked them together as he presented their earnestness as an example for the encouragement of the disciples in Corinth.

Provinces Linked Together

The bond widens to include churches in many provinces, and once again they are linked together, for Peter addressed his letter to "to those who are elect exiles of the Dispersion in Pontus, Galatia, Cappadocia, Asia, and Bithynia." This must have included many churches, and not only were they linked together, but the elders were also, for Peter writes to them as one: "I exhort the elders among you" (1 Peter 5:1).

You will notice he refers to the flock of God which was among them – not flocks in the plural, but one flock. Each elder had a charge allotted to him, and he would have a special care for that part of the flock which comprised his home assembly but the whole flock was one. Then please consider with me the striking word in Acts 9:31: "the church throughout all Judea and Galilee and Samaria had peace and was being built up. And walking in the fear of the Lord and in the comfort of the Holy Spirit, it multiplied." That was the full extent of the work at the time, for the word had not reached beyond those three provinces. Can you see that the whole movement was one?

The church throughout the three provinces was otherwise described as "the church of the living God, the pillar and buttress of the truth" (1 Timothy 3:15). And so it continued to be as the work grew. A few churches were linked together in a province and another few in another province as the work expanded, and all the provinces in turn joined together so that the whole movement was one. Is not that the lesson of the ten curtains of the tabernacle? Some have expressed surprise that we should see in so small a detail a lesson for us today. But why? If the God of creation has given careful attention to such tiny details as the stamen of a flower or the sting of a bee, producing them in such wonderful perfection, should we be surprised when He gives attention to detail in something so important as His dwelling place among His people?

We have no doubt whatever that the churches of God in the New Testament were linked together and that the unity which resulted was exceedingly precious to God. The One who linked them by His word is seen in Revelation chapter 1 walking among those churches. Just seven actual churches of God; not just symbols of church ages; and perhaps the only ones left, but still very precious to Him despite the sin and failure which had crept in. "I will make my dwelling among them, and walk among them" (2 Corinthians 6:16) was His earlier promise, and there He is still, Son over God's house a message for each of the churches. How He loved them and cared for them!

We hear the cry rising from the heart of the great Intercessor as He pleaded with His Father for the men He was leaving behind, and for those, down through the centuries of time, who would believe on Him through their word (John 17:20, 21). The churches that were brought together as a result of that word became the special target of the great adversary. We are not surprised at that - if God set such value on them the devil would do his utmost to disrupt them.

One of his tactics was to introduce false doctrine. It was because of false teaching brought to Antioch by some men from Judea that the apostles and elders met for the historic conference in Jerusalem which Acts 15 describes in detail. As a result of the apostles and elders conferring together under the direction of the Holy Spirit they reached agreement on the point which had disturbed the disciples in Antioch. "It has seemed good to the Holy Spirit and to us ..." they wrote. Decrees were issued and put in writing and they became binding, not in Antioch alone, but on all the churches. It plainly says "as they went on their way through the cities, they delivered to them for observance the decisions that had been reached by the apostles and elders who were in Jerusalem. So the churches were strengthened in the faith, and they increased in numbers daily" (Acts 16:4,5).

Does that not present to us a clear line of teaching? Not only does it show that the churches were linked together as one, all bound by the same decrees, but also that their unity was maintained by elders conferring and acting together. And by way of testimony we might add that for over 100 years we have found it to be very effective. Time and again issues of doctrine and practice have threatened to divide us and may well have done so, had it not been for a regular conference of representative overseers from all the churches of God, convened on the pattern of Acts 15.

There under the guidance of God's gracious Spirit, oneness of mind has been reached and we have gone on together. "Behold, how good and pleasant it is when brothers dwell in unity" (Psalm 133:1). It is indeed, and we are assured that by a united elderhood working together in harmony it can be achieved. Some have contended that the example of Acts 15 was an isolated case and it is true there is only one recorded conference of elders and that at a time when the apostles were still with them. But is that one, spelled out in such detail, not sufficient to guide us in our doctrine and practice today? We believe it is, and that God has

29

placed it on the page of scripture for that very purpose.

Review

1. The Lord Jesus in His prayer in John 17, three times re-peated "That they may all be one." Can you show from Scripture that this unity can only be attained by each disciple obeying the word of the Lord?
2. How would you show from Scripture that (a) the churches of God were grouped together in districts or provinces, and (b) the provinces were linked together in one Fellowship?
3. How was this unity maintained?

GOD'S PATTERN FOR TODAY

"**B**ut where are the churches of God you are speaking about?" some ask. "How are we to recognise them?" The question is a proper one, for many groups of Christians call themselves by the same name, but when their doctrines are examined it is evident they believe and practise many different things. So we must stop at this point and make clear what we mean when we refer to present-day churches of God. Indeed we must get back to God's word and find out what the characteristics were of a New Testament church of God.

The first church of God was in Jerusalem, brought into being on the day of Pentacost. When Peter preached his sermon that day the Spirit of God worked in the hearts of about 3000 people. Acts 2:41,42 refers to them when it says, "So those who received his word were baptized, and there were added that day about three thousand souls. And they devoted themselves to the apostles' teaching and the fellowship, to the breaking of bread and the prayers." There are seven distinct things mentioned in those verses which might be viewed as seven pillars on which a church of God is built. Certainly they are seven characteristics by which a church of God can be identified.

Seven Features of a Church of God

They **received His word** and by that word they were saved. "Whoever hears my word and believes him who sent me has eternal life," the Lord Jesus said (John 5:24) and so it was on Pentecost day. By the operation of the Holy Spirit through the word of God they were born again.

They were **baptized**. This was baptism by immersion in water, and it followed their salvation. It was not in order to be saved, but because they were saved. Similarly "many of the Corinthians, hearing Paul, believed and were baptized" (Acts 18:8). They were baptized in obedience to the word of the Lord Jesus and as a declaration of the fact that they were His disciples.

Then the baptized disciples were **added** to those already to-gether, of whom Acts 1:15 speaks. So in the church of God in Jerusalem it was known who was in the church and who was not. Those inside had been added by the Lord (Acts 2:47). In the language of 1 Peter 2 they were the living stones built together into a building for God. And we can see at once it was not for occasional fellowship, but a lifetime commitment. When of Tarsus came to Jerusalem after his conversion he tried to join the disciples, and the word translated 'join' here the sense of something permanant. And this is emphasised by the fact that they continued steadfastly.

The **apostles' teaching** embraces the whole of our New Testa-ment. It originated with their Master, for He committed large parts of it to them before He returned to heaven. Other parts were delivered directly to the apostle Paul by the Lord from heaven: "I received from the Lord what I also delivered to you" (1 Corinthians 11:23). The early disciples obviously accepted it as binding upon them, and in it they continued steadfastly. They also continued steadfastly in fellowship, a fellowship of those who were prepared to acknowledge the Lordship of Christ, and as we see from 1 Corinthians 1:9 it belonged to Him; it was the fellowship of God's Son and in churches of God they enjoyed fellowship with Him and with His Father, and also with one another, for they were "together, and had all things in common" (Acts 2:44).

They continued steadfastly also in the **breaking of bread.** This was the weekly remembrance of the Lord Jesus in obedience to His word, "This do in remembrance of me." It was a function of the church of God as 1 Corinthians 11:20,22 makes clear and they gathered together as a church (v.18) in order to keep that remembrance. That it was kept each Lord's day is plain from such scriptures as Acts 20:7 and 1 Corinthians 16:2, for at that time they brought to the Lord their money gifts as well as their spiritual sacrifices, making confession to His name (1 Peter 2:5, Hebrews 13:15).

Finally, they continued also in the **prayers.** Not individual prayer in this case (other passages stress the importance of that), but the prayers of the church. They gathered themselves together in order to pray and they did so on a regular basis as well as on special occasions as Acts 12:5 envisages. The prayer meetings of that first church of God were powerful occasions, resulting in great power in the apostles' witness of the resurrection of the Lord Jesus, and in great grace being upon them all.

You will agree that these seven things are each of fundamental importance. The local testimony was built upon them, and by means of them the church of God in each town or city became a witness to the truth of God which they held. The order of the seven steps is important too. God has given us His order and it is all part of the pattern to which we must build. If we alter it, even in one way, can we claim to be a church of God, part of the one house in which He is served? In the Old Testament God was most particular about the detail of His pattern. And our New Testament scriptures would lead us to believe He is no less particular today.

God Speaks through Ezekiel

Christian, have you measured the pattern? In Ezekiel 43:10 (Revised Version) where God is speaking about His house of the future, Ezekiel writes "Let them measure the pattern." In the future, God's house will be built again, a physical house once more: "the mountain of the house of the Lord shall be established as the highest of the mountains ... and all the nations shall flow to it," (Isaiah 2:2). And of that house God says he "will set my sanctuary in their midst forevermore. My dwelling place shall be with them, and I will be their God, and they shall be my people" (Ezekiel 37:26,27).

Once again all the principles we have been considering together will be fulfilled and God invites them to measure the pattern, and to take note that everything is according to His word. We cannot read these chapters in Ezekiel without sensing the great pleasure God will derive from it. "He said to me, "Son of man, this is the place of my throne and the place of the soles of my feet'" (Ezekiel 43:7).

Some believers are unconcerned about this glorious truth of God dwelling with people on earth. Would you be willing to measure the pattern - to take the pattern of God's word and place it alongside what you have been practising? For example, examine your breaking of bread service. Are unbaptized believers allowed to take part? If so, can it be right? When faced with that question some immediately react by saying, "But you can't deny any of God's children the right to come to the Father's table!" But is it the Father's table? Is that the apostles' teaching? Nowhere is it referred to in that way in the Scriptures.

1 Corinthians 10:21 distinctly says it is the table of the Lord, and once again we are back to the subject of the Lordship of Christ and the obedience His Lordship demands of us. Look at the subject of adding, which is so often misunderstood and sometimes ignored altogether. The result is that many fail to appreciate the concept of a church of God composed of disciples added together, and instead they just "come to church" without any sense of belonging to it. And without adding, how can there be discipline and government in God's house? "Let them measure the pattern." The Lord is speaking. It is His invitation. Would you be willing to do that? It is well worth it if God is leading you to the place of His choice.

Review

1. The Church of God in Jerusalem was characterised by each disciple having followed seven steps. Which of the seven were a once-only experience, and which were ongoing?

2. Why was the sequence important?

3. They form part of 'the pattern of sound words' which Timothy was urged to hold (2 Timothy 1:13). God speaks about measuring the pattern. How do we do this?

"WHOSE HOUSE ARE WE, IF WE HOLD FAST"

"But I've always thought all believers together compose God's house," you may say. Many born-again people do believe that, and sincerely so. We must therefore give thought to this point of view. It is true that the redeemed body of each believer is a dwelling place of God, for God's Spirit lives in us: "Do you not know that your body is a temple of the Holy Spirit within you, whom you have from God?" (1 Corinthians 6:19). This is a precious truth. But we are considering now a people together as a dwelling place for God and the question before us is, can all believers on earth at any one time answer to this concept of God's house on earth?

In Matthew 16 when Peter made his confession of faith in Christ as the Son of the living God, the Lord Jesus spoke for the first time about the church which He was to build. "On this rock [of Peter's confession as to His eternal deity] I will build My church; and the gates of Hades shall not prevail against it," He said. He began the building of that church on the day of Pentecost when the Holy Spirit descended to fill believing hearts. It is referred to as "the church, which is his body" (Ephesians 1:22,23). It comprises all believers in the Lord Jesus from that day of the

Spirit's outpouring to the day when Christ shall return for His own, and then His church will be complete.

It is an eternal thing, so that those who die in Christ are still members of it. And it is indestructible, the gates of Hades not being able to prevail against it, so that once a member is built into it by Christ Himself, he is in it for ever. It is Christ's own church and every one of us who believes in our Lord Jesus is very thankful to be a member of it.

Two Distinct Movements

But on that same day of Pentecost another movement began. For those who were saved as a result of Peter's preaching and became members of Christ's own church, were then baptized in water in obedience to Christ's word, and Acts 2:42 says they were added to those already together in what is described as the church of God in Jerusalem (see Galatians 1:13 and Acts 8:1). Into the Church, His Body they were placed (or baptized in the Spirit) when they accepted Christ as Saviour. Into the church of God they were added after they had been baptized in water in acknowledgement of Christ as Lord.

The basis of membership in Christ's Church, His Body was faith in Him. But obedience to His word was the basis of fellowship in a church of God. We can see then that two movements began that day. They were closely related to one another and yet distinct. The one Christ was building was eternal and heavenly; the other belonged to the earth. It had to do with the members of Christ's Body bearing witness together locally as a church of God in their own town or city for as long as they lived, and when they died they ceased to be part of it.

Also, if they were to continue in churches of God in testimony to God's truth along with others, there required to be continuing obedience on their part to His word. In 1 Corinthians 5 we read of a brother who lost his place in the church of God because of immorality. "Let him who has done this be removed from among you" was the apostolic instruction. He was still a member of the Body of Christ but until he repented of his sin (as 2 Corinthians 2:6-8 seems to indicate he did) he was outside the local testimony for God. We can see, therefore, that whereas membership of the Church His Body is an unconditional thing, dependent only upon our initial faith in Christ as Saviour, a disciple's place in a church of God is very much dependent upon his or her continuing obedience to the Lord's word.

A Lesson from Shiloh

Indeed, the churches of God as a whole continue to be God's house only as long as there is amongst them continuing obedience to His word. There came a time when God forsook His house in Shiloh. "He forsook his dwelling at Shiloh, the tent where He dwelt among mankind" (Psalm 78:60). The story makes sad reading. Days of spiritual decline followed Israel's settling in the land, leading eventually to complete disregard of His word. But the patience of God waited, even when the priests who served in His house were men of extreme wickedness. It was still His house as long as His presence was there. And while it remained so, He valued highly such acts of devotion as Hannah showed when she brought her young son and loaned him to the Lord for as long as he lived.

39

In God's house he served, a young unblemished life amidst so much corruption. But the time came when the glory of God departed. We cannot fail to see the link with Hebrews 3:6: "Christ is faithful over God's house as a son. And we are his house, if indeed we hold fast our confidence and our boasting in our hope." God dwelling among men on earth has always been conditional on their obedience to His word. When that fails, it is only a question of time, in the forbearance of God, before the presence of the Lord has departed.

If we grasp the distinction between these two movements it is surely not difficult to see that all believers do not, and could not, compose God's house, although it is the will of God that they should. They do compose the church His Body (together with those who have died in Christ) but the house of God is a place of service and witness, where there is a pattern of teaching to be held (2 Timothy 1:13) and obeyed from the heart (Romans 6:17). The "all" of Christ's commanding are to be observed (Matthew 28:20) and the faith once for all delivered to the saints to be earnestly contended for (Jude 3). Human responsibility is emphasised in each case.

Things Which Differ

There are things which differ in the word of God and the Holy Spirit will teach us to differentiate between them. In stressing the truth of God's house we are not overlooking the most precious truth that "you all are one in Christ Jesus" (Galatians 3:28). In the Body of Christ there is a unity which is indestructible and we are conscious of it every time we meet another Christian. How close are the bonds which bind us together! But the New Testament churches were not formed on the basis of unity in Christ, but on the ground of obedience to the Lord.

Notice as just one example of this the opening words of the first Corinthian epistle: "To the church of God that is in Corinth, to those sanctified in Christ Jesus, called to be saints together with all those who in every place call upon the name of our Lord Jesus Christ, both their Lord and ours." And calling upon Him as Lord demands obedience to His word. "Why do you call me, 'Lord, Lord', and do not do what I tell you?" (Luke 6:46). To many believers this seems harsh. They prefer the gentler approach of all being one in Christ. "Let's forget our differences" they say, "and enjoy our common love in Christ."

It sounds pleasant, but it does not work out in practice. The result, to a large extent, is that every man does what is right in his own eyes (Judges 21:25) and the scattering of Christians in so many different denominations is evidence that this is so. We once again appeal to you to face the challenge of God's word. How could all believers together possibly compose God's house when so many are holding different beliefs and practising different things? "God is not a God of confusion but of peace; as in all the churches of the saints ..." (1 Corinthians 14:33). The churches of God were churches of the saints as to their composition. Those saints were disciples of the Lord Jesus as 1 Corinthians 1:2 shows, bound together by the love of Christ for one another but also by obedience to Christ's word.

When those same churches are linked together in a unity, is this not something which the world can see? And does it not answer to the request in our Master's prayer in John 17:21 "that they may all be one, just as You, Father, are in Me, and I in You; that they also may be in us, so that the world may believe that You have sent Me"?

Review

1. Using two columns, list some of the differences between The Church which is Christ's Body and The Church and Churches of God. Some Bible teachers have found 15 differences. How many can you find? For example: There is one Body (Ephesians 4:4), but there are many churches of God (2 Thessalonians 1:4); Christ is the Builder of the Body (Matthew 16:18), but men build the Church of God, (1 Corinthians 3:10); The Church the Body is indestructible (Matthew 16:18), but the Church of God may be destroyed (Galatians 1:13).

2. Why did God forsake His first house at Shiloh?

3. What is the difference between the expressions "in Christ" or "in Christ Jesus" (as in Galatians 3:28) and "in the Lord" (as in 1 Thessalonians 5:12)?

"THE DAY OF SMALL THINGS"

"That's just presumption! To claim that your churches form the house of God when you're such a small people. That's a proud claim. How can it be?" The speaker was a Christian friend of mine in South India. We were on good terms and could speak freely together without causing offence. Hence his outspokenness. "But Bill, you tell me there are between 700 and 800 million people in India and less than 2 per cent are Christians. Is it presumptuous for an Indian who believes in the Lord Jesus to call himself a child of God to the exclusion of all other Indians?"

"Oh no," he replied, "of course not, for the word of God says so." "Yes, and that's the point I'm making. Acting on what God says isn't presumption, nor should it be construed as pride. If the word of God clearly indicates both a way and a place in which God wants us to serve Him, surely it is not wrong to put into practice what God shows us." Those who comprise the present day churches of God and who make up our Fellowship are a comparatively small people, but for over 125 years we have been sending out our message, praying that other believers will search their Bibles to see if these things are so. And if so, to stand with us in proclaiming these truths of His word. In that spirit we send out our message once again. We love all our fellow-believers, members with us, and we with them, of the Body of Christ. We have the same Father in heaven, and are destined to share His glorious home together. We thank God for what each one is doing to make Christ known in a world so fiercely opposed to Him.

But that does not mean that when we see parts of His word still to be obeyed we should hold back because other Christians do not see it the same way. We are answerable to our Lord Jesus. We must obey His word. One day we shall stand before Him to give an account of our service. And we believe obedience to His word will weigh heavily then. We write out of deep conviction that the subject of His dwelling among men is very near and dear to the heart of God. The boy Jesus came into His house at the age of twelve, and to the wondering question of His mother He replied, "Did you not know that I must be in my Father's house?" (Luke 2:49). Into it He came again as a man and seeing it turned into a market, the zeal of God's house consumed Him as He overthrew the money changers' tables and drove out the animals.

He knew, above all others, how much this house meant to God, and He loved it with all His heart. Shall we not love it too, and stand together for the truth of it, and live to serve God in it?

An Illustration

Such thoughts as God's love for His dwelling place must have filled the hearts of the men and women who left Babylon to return to Jerusalem to rebuild God's house. We read of them in the early chapters of Ezra. Seventy years before, the Babylonians had plundered the magnificent temple which Solomon had built for God, breaking down the carved work with hatchet and hammers, and setting the sanctuary on fire (Psalm 74:6,7). Their home was now in Babylon but they were God's people nevertheless and some of them could scarcely contain their joy when the news spread through the land that Cyrus the king was actually encouraging them to return and rebuild God's house in Jerusalem. It seemed too good to be true.

"Then our mouth was filled with laughter, and our tongue with shouts of joy" (Psalm 126:2). God was behind it, of course. It was He who stirred the heart of Cyrus. The 70 years of captivity He had decreed were up and it was time to return and build. But who would go? That was the question. Most of the people had been born in Babylon and life was comfortable there. Why uproot themselves and go to a land they did not know? There was only one valid reason for so great an upheaval. Jerusalem was the place of the Name. God's house was there, lying in ruins.

So the issue was the same as we face today. What about God's house? Does the truth of it so grip our hearts that we are prepared, if need be, to make some sacrifice, first of all to be associated with it ourselves and then to serve in it according to the instruction of God's word? Those were stirring days under the leadership of Zerubbabel and Joshua the high priest. Not only did God stir the heart of the heathen king, He stirred the hearts of Israel's leaders too, and of the people. And 42,360 of them decided to go. God numbers them, down to the last one, in Ezra chapter 2, as though every single one of them was precious to Him. Of course they were. Leaving home and security and in many cases their loved ones, they went out to a land most of them did not know One purpose inspired all their hearts - to rebuild God's house.

God's Prophets Speak

42,360 of them! Just a remnant compared with the number taken captive 70 years before. And so few compared with all who could have gone had they so desired. But what did that matter? It was every man whose heart made him willing. And with willing hearts they went, and gave, and worked until eventually God's house was rebuilt and its service begun again. It did not happen without discouragements and setbacks, all of which the book of Ezra records for our instruction. And along with the historical account in Ezra we need to read the prophecies of Haggai and Zechariah, for God sent these two prophets at that time to encourage the people forward. Without their help the work may never have been completed.

When the foundation was laid the old men wept, for they compared it with the glory of Solomon's temple. The thing looked so small in comparison. But God's word through Zechariah was "Whoever has despised the day of small things?" (Zechariah 4:10). Certainly God did not despise it. On the contrary, His word through Haggai was, "Go up to the hills and bring wood and build the house, that I may take pleasure in it and that I may be glorified, says the LORD" (Haggai 1:8). Could they have desired anything greater than that? If it was for God's glory, and to give Him pleasure, was it not worth devoting their whole lives to the task? Was any sacrifice on their part too great?

"That I may take pleasure in it." In what? This small thing they were building? Yes, that was what God said. It was small, and it was only made of wood, but that did not matter to God. It was the obedience of their hearts He valued. To dwell again among a people who loved Him sufficiently to obey His word was something exceedingly precious to God. We have noticed, have we not, that it always has been so from the days of Moses, when the people first built for Him. And surely it is so today, as we build God's spiritual house. We are few and the thing is comparatively small, as is evident to all who take time to look at it. But is it to the pattern? And does God take pleasure in it?

An Appeal

To all my Christian friends who have patiently followed with me through this booklet thus far, let us examine our Bibles carefully to see if these things are so. The Beroeans have left us a good example in this, for it is recorded, "They received the word with all eagerness, examining the Scriptures daily to see if these things were so" (Acts 17:11). The Holy Spirit has been given to guide us into all truth. Let us seek His help to direct us in this also. And as He gives us assurance in our hearts let us join together in building a place where God may rest according to His heart's desire and where we may serve according to the pattern of His word.

Review

1. Suggest a reason why God takes the time to list and number all those who left Babylon to rebuild His house in Jerusalem?
2. Why did the old men weep when the foundation was laid?

3. "That I may take pleasure in it" God said about this rebuilt temple. If His house on earth gave Him so much pleasure then, can you think of a reason for God feeling the same about His spiritual house today?

"A TREASURE OF MY OWN"

"O LORD, I love the habitation of your house, and the place where Your glory dwells" (Psalm 26:8). So said King David. And the record of his life is proof of the truth of his words. When he came to the throne of Israel at 30 years of age his first thoughts were for the ark of God. It had been forgotten and neglected by the people as a whole during the reign of King Saul. One of the first things David did was to bring it up and pitch a tent for it in his own city (1 Chronicles 16:1).

But the tabernacle was in Gibeon, so the service of God was divided. Years before, God had foreseen this happening and He spoke of "an enemy in my habitation" (1 Samuel 2:32, Revised Version). David obviously sensed God's feeling about it, for he said, "Remember, O Lord, in David's favor, all the hardships he endured, how he swore to the Lord and vowed to the Mighty One of Jacob, 'I will not enter my house or get into my bed, I will not give sleep to my eyes or slumber to my eyelids, until I find a place for the Lord, a dwelling place for the Mighty One of Jacob'" (Psalm 132:1-5).

How very precious! God's affliction was David's affliction. If ever a man's heart beat true to God it was David's. He told Nathan the prophet of his great desire to build God a house; and back again through Nathan came God's gentle though negative reply. He spoke of His deep appreciation of David's desire, and the fact that because he had been a man of war the honour of building His house was to go instead to his son. David accepted God's decision and set about making preparation for it, and typical of the man, he put all his heart into it. The 29th chapter of 1 Chronicles makes touching reading.

David had come to the close of his life and was handing over responsibility to his son, Solomon. Reviewing his life of service he said "I have provided for the house of my God, so far as I was able, the gold for the things of gold, the silver for the things of silver, and the bronze for the things of bronze, the iron for the things of iron, and wood for the things of wood, besides great quantities of onyx and stones for setting, antimony, colored stones, all sorts of precious stones and marble. Moreover, in addition to all that I have provided for the holy house, I have a treasure of my own of gold and silver and because of my devotion to the house of my God I give it to the house of my God" (1 Chronicles 29:2-4).

Both strength and love had motivated him in his task, even to the point of giving his own special treasure. It was something specially his own, to give or to withhold. How greatly God must have valued that sacrifice. His example inspired others and when the call rang out, "Who then is willing to consecrate himself this day to the LORD?" (1 Chronicles 29:5, Revised Version) there was a great response. Princes, captains and rulers all filled their hands with gifts and offered themselves willingly to advance the great work of building a house for God, as worthy of His Name as they could make it. Those were heart-stirring days.

Another Leader, Another Day

We pass on to consider another day, and another outstanding leader in the service of God. From the moment Saul met the living Christ on the road to Damascus his life was completely yielded to Him. He had a treasure of his own, too - a life to give, and he gave it without reserve. "What shall I do, Lord?" was the cry which rang from his heart the day he met Christ, and having been told what the Lord required of him, he set himself to do it, utterly and completely. In tireless energy and without regard to the sacrifice and suffering involved he laboured to finish his task.

"To spend and be spent" was an expression he used of his own glad service, for he did not account his life of any value or precious to himself, that he might finish his course and the ministry he had received from the Lord Jesus (Acts 20:24). And what was this ministry? Acts 26:16-18 sums it up and the words deserve our careful examination. We see it included the preaching of the gospel and also bringing his converts to an inheritance which would become theirs by obedience to the word of God (compare Acts 20:32). This is not the inheritance in heaven which belongs to all those who are born again, of which 1 Peter 1:4 speaks, but rather an inheritance on earth which brings a person into the service of God within His house. As in David's case, so with Saul (now the apostle Paul); his example inspired others, and there was gathered around him a band of like-minded men who became his companions in service, his "fellow-workers unto the kingdom of God."

It makes stirring reading to follow the apostle and his companions as they carried out the work of God on those three missionary journeys which we have come to link with the name of the apostle Paul. Their service kept to a consistent pattern as they pursued their task, always outward and onward with their message that God "desires all people to be saved and to come to the knowledge of the truth" (1 Timothy 2:4). Let us take their work at Corinth as an example. Reaching that cosmopolitan Greek city, famous as a centre of commerce and learning, Paul began by preaching the gospel. In himself he felt weak and fearful, as he later confided, but the power of the Spirit clothed his preaching of Jesus Christ.

And when some believed "he stayed a year and six months, teaching the word of God among them" (Acts 18:11). And those who were responsive to the teaching were gathered together into a church of God, which he described as "God's building" (1 Corinthians 3:9). Three main roles he filled: preacher, teacher, and church-builder; the one work leading to the other. And before the wise master-builder passed on to his next place of labour, he had laid a foundation and built upon it such people as were obedient to the commandments of the risen Christ. On that foundation the obedient ones were then left to build.

The Pattern of Service

So in addition to the pattern of teaching there was also a pattern of service. Preaching, teaching, building; it was the same in every place. And as they journeyed ever onward, they left behind them a growing number of churches of God, lampstands all of gold, as Revelation 1 pictures them, sending out amidst the darkness the light of divine truth. But if that light was to shine undimmed it would depend upon the disciples who composed the churches living holy lives. Of this the beloved apostle was well aware and very much of the teaching in his epistles had to do with holy living and behaviour, both in individual lives and in their testimony together in churches of God.

When he wrote his first letter to Timothy he was nearing the end of his service and his early vision of God's house was as clear as ever: "I hope to come to you soon, but I am writing these things to you so that, if I delay, you may know how one ought to behave in the household of God, which is the church of the living God, a pillar and buttress of the truth" (1 Timothy 3:14-15). In the previous chapters, Paul had been dealing with the role of men and women in the churches of God, and that of overseers and deacons.

Truth Personified

Then he concluded the passage with that sublime verse, "He was manifested in the flesh, vindicated by the Spirit, seen by angels, proclaimed among the nations, believed on in the world taken up in glory. (1 Timothy 3:16). Do you see the connection? When the Lord Jesus was on earth His life was the very embodiment of truth. "Truth is in Jesus," says Paul in Ephesians 4:21. In that perfect life He lived, the truth of God shone out in all its perfection. But now He has returned to heaven, where should the light of God's truth be seen? The answer is, in the lives of disciples, indwelt by the Holy Spirit whose gracious work is to transform those very people from glory to glory, and to produce in them a likeness to God's holy Son.

But not to individuals shining on their own is this portion referring, precious and important though that is, but to disciples together in churches of God, shining as lamps on a lampstand, and those churches in aggregate combining to form God's house. This is the pillar and ground of the truth. Do you not catch that vision? And would you not like to translate it into your life? You also have a treasure of your own, a life to give and to live for God's glory. "I have given to the house of my God ... my own special treasure," said David (Revised Version). "I do not account my life of any value nor as precious to myself, if only I may finish my course and the ministry that I received from the Lord Jesus," said the apostle Paul. Wise men! Their examples inspire us still. Who among us shall be prepared to do the same?

Review

1. Two vital ways in which David provided for the building of the temple were (a) by inspiring other leaders with his love and zeal for God's house, and (b) by passing to his son the pattern of the house received from God. What was a third way?

2. Paul spoke of the ministry he had received from the Lord Jesus (Acts 20:24). Name three areas of service included in that ministry.

3. 'Oh, send out Your light and Your truth' (Psalm 43:3). Notice from the psalm how that light and truth shines out from God's house. Can you identify how the holy living of disciples in churches of God is vital for the fulfilment of

that prayer?

EPILOGUE

I f you have patiently followed to this point, you will realise that this booklet is written especially for Bible-loving Christians who sincerely desire to follow the Lord completely in their lives. The pattern of churches of God, linked in the fellowship of the Son of God, was clear in New Testament times, from Pentecost onwards. It had its roots in the tabernacle and the temples in Jerusalem in Old Testament days. But it is not so clear today, with a proliferation of Christian churches, each with its own interpretation of particular scriptures. Such variety of denominations cannot be of God, who desires unity among believers, without compromising His truth. It is necessary today, therefore, for disciples of the Lord Jesus to search for the truth among so much confusion.

Unfortunately, some sincere Christians feel that such a search is relatively unimportant because we are all one in Christ Jesus. Others feel that it is divisive and sectarian. But a careful reading of Scripture, in both Testaments, makes it clear that these are not unimportant details, but truths dear to God's heart, although hidden to many. Is it not possible to get back to the simple New Testament pattern and put it into practice? We believe it is. Over 125 years ago (in the 1890s) there was a movement of God's Spirit in the hearts of certain men and women who saw this pattern in their Bibles but realized they were falling short of it in what they were building.

For the most part they were joined with others in the 'Brethren movement' which since 1830 God had used for the recovery of many precious truths. But they were convinced there was more truth to be grasped and obeyed. The churches of God should be one, linked together in a divine unity, and kept together by means of united elders. So they taught these truths and published them in a magazine called 'Needed Truth' (https://churchesofgod.info/publications/nt-archive) to draw attention to them. Finally they realized that the only way they could put them into practice was by separating from their brethren. It was a high price to pay, for many were saying goodbye to good friends whom they loved and with whom they had served for many years. But the call of God was on them.

The Spirit of God was moving them and they must obey Him, so there came into being again the churches of God in the fellowship of the Son of God. By God's gracious help these have continued to this present day, bearing witness to the whole of God's truth, and in particular to this important subject of God dwelling among men. So to any who seek after God's house, we are able to say there exist again today churches of God, linked worldwide under a united elderhood, a revival under God, we firmly believe, of the spiritual house of God as seen in the New Testament. If it is your longing to be found where God dwells among His people on earth, a people worshipping and serving according to His clear pattern, then we appeal to you to write to us so that we may communicate further with you on this vital subject.

Review

What was the main line of God's truth which persuaded godly men and women in the 1890s to separate from the Brethren movement so that they could give expression to it in churches of God?

ABOUT THE PUBLISHER

Hayes Press (www.hayespress.org) is a registered charity in the United Kingdom, whose primary mission is to disseminate the Word of God, mainly through literature. It is one of the largest distributors of gospel tracts and leaflets in the United Kingdom, with over 100 titles and many thousands dispatched annually. In addition to paperbacks and eBooks, Hayes Press also publishes Plus Eagles' Wings, a fun and educational Bible magazine for children, and Golden Bells, a popular daily Bible reading calendar in wall or desk formats.

If you would like to contact Hayes Press, there are a number of ways you can do so:

By mail: c/o The Barn, Flaxlands, Royal Wootton Bassett, Wiltshire, UK SN4 8DY

By phone: 01793 850598

By eMail:info@hayespress.org

via Facebook: www.facebook.com/hayespress.org

MORE BOOKS FROM HAYES PRESS

Uncovering the Pattern: God's Way of Unity for Disciples Today

There are hundreds of Christian denominations today, all teaching and practicing different things - is this really God's plan? This book explains how God reveals to us in the Bible how He wants all Christians to serve Him: Part 1 explores how God's purposes are ultimately collective and not just with individuals; Part 2 reviews how God works through covenants - firstly the Old and then the New; Part 3 looks at the important differences between the Church the Body and the Churches of God in scripture; Part 4 brings it back to the personal level and our personal accountability to act on what God has shown us from His Word.

Back To Basics: A Study of Core Bible Teaching and Practice

This book uses a combination of theological and practical content and study questions to explore 8 key topics that are essential to the Christian faith: Knowing God, Salvation, Believer's Baptism, The Breaking of Bread, Understanding The Bible, The Return of Jesus Christ, Spiritual Gifts and Church Life.

1.The Trinity - Theology (David Viles)
2.God in my Life - Practical (Karl Smith)
3.Eternally Secure Salvation - Theology (Craig Jones)
4.Taking Hold – Practical (Richard Hutchinson)
5.Baptism of Believers - Theology (Alex Reid)
6.Walking in Newness of Life - Practical (Stephen Hickling)
7.The Lord's Supper - Theology (James Needham)
8.Do This Until I Come - Practical (Don Williamson)
9.The Bible – Theology (David Viles)
10.Reading the Bible for All It's Worth - Practical (Karl Smith)
11.The Lord's Return - Theology (Craig Jones)
12.He's Coming Soon - Practical (David Woods)
13.Spiritual Gifts - Theology (Alex Reid)
14.Using our Gifts to God's Glory - Practical (Stephen Hickling)
15.The Church and Churches of God - Theology (James Needham)
16.Living to God's Pattern - Practical (Don Williamson)

With study questions for each of the 8 topics as an appendix, this book is ideal for personal or group study.